A Memoir ... So Far

True stories about falling down and getting
back up

Carol L Beers

ISBN

Paperback: 979-8-90190-068-0

Hardcover: 979-8-90190-069-7

Emotions on Sharing My Life Story

It seems like I've always had stories to tell. With a large family and 24 nieces and nephews and triplet aunts and uncles who seem to hear some of the stories and ask to hear them again probably because they're unbelievable until they ask around and find out they're true.

My first memory was in Detroit, Michigan where we lived. My 2 sisters (the oldest one, Terry, and the younger one, Linda) and our Mom and Dad. It was my sister Terry's first day of school in kindergarten, and mom said I could walk her there and come straight back. When we got there, Terry couldn't wait and ran to open the huge gate, turned her back, slammed it fast, and ran into school! I yelled goodbye, but I don't think she even heard me. I grabbed the big gate, but it was already closed and locked. With tears in my eyes (I missed the age deadline by 4 days), I slowly walked the whole way back home all alone.

After lunch, I waited and waited, and then I remembered the Lone Ranger Show. I decided to see if I could hear her coming, so I leaned down on the sidewalk and listened to see if I could hear her footsteps. Wouldn't you know, a huge black ant ran right into my ear! I chased it with my finger and could NOT get it out. It was time for drastic measures. I had thought up too many bad endings and decided to see if I could get some help. This day was not going well. I ran all the way back home into our house and found my mom just getting up from her nap with Linda by her side. I could hardly see with tears in my eyes once again; she immediately got it out of my ear with cotton and a flashlight. I knew the vacuum was next, so I was so relieved when suddenly I was saved by 2 beautiful long arms picking me up, hugging me carefully, and her beautiful loving face with the strangest smile. She didn't know yet about listening for the footsteps. I felt so lucky to be able to wait another year to learn stuff at school and to see that learning early lessons are important even if it's trial and error and when to go get help even though it was only a big old ant.

Terry, Carol and Linda

First Glimpses:
Painting a Picture of Life in My Early Years

Another time in my early memories was with my little brother Dean and cousin Donnie. I think we were 8, 6, and 5 in a new neighborhood in Detroit. It was a beautiful day, and we were off to the "Mississippi River" (really just across and down the street). There was a tall house being built on a construction site. It was deserted and quiet, and to our delight, a very long ladder tilted up to the roof!

The boys said we should go up to see which way the "river" was. Since I was the oldest, I said okay but to be very careful and not mess around.

After helping them get started and making sure not to look down, I closely followed them climbing slowly after them straight upward. I watched them reach the top and talked them through getting from the ladder to their hands and knees on the roof, then resting with all three of us on our butts.

After a minute, we started walking around and they were yelling for me to hurry up. I thought there was something wrong. I asked where the river was, and they were both crying and started yelling for me to look down below! Some mean man had pushed the ladder down, got in his car, and drove away! We sat down and tried to figure out a plan. First, we tried yelling and screaming, but no one heard. Then we tried to throw stuff. Nothing was working, and we could see all of us had worry on our faces.

When I came up with a plan to see where the lowest place on the roof was and the boys delighted in letting me know they figured out I was the tallest one and it was only three of me to the ground (it would be four or five of them to the ground). Now I realize how important math is! After a few more really ridiculous plans that included sleeping up on the roof, I thought I should not worry about figuring anything out. So, I kneeled near the edge the boys showed me. I got down on my knees and hung on to the edge of the roof and lifted my body over and just released. I landed just right in a pile of sand. The plan worked.

When I finally got up and brushed off all the dirt, I realized I didn't die and nothing was broken. I remembered in a TV show Timmie was about to fall from a tree limb, Lassie started barking, and a man heard and followed with a tall ladder and saved them. I started dragging our ladder just like the man on TV so I could push it up rung by rung against the house. It seemed to take forever, but I finally got the ladder where it needed to be.

I was on the ground holding the bottom and talked the youngest, my cousin Donnie, through backing down one step at a time. To my surprise, he got the hang of it and slowly walked with his front facing the house and my little brother Dean holding the top. Then Dean came down just like Donnie, and we all did a crazy dance and cried a few more happy tears and pushed the monster ladder down to the ground where it should have been in the first place.

We swore we would never tell, but we couldn't help it, and there was no dessert after supper but a great story to tell. My Dad decided to have us take him over to the house, and he had a talk with the man in the car. I swear the arms were flying, but no fights broke out! We were all very lucky and told the family about figuring out some plans on the top of the roof of the house and did the math and didn't panic... well, maybe just a little, and it really pays off to stay calm together.

Also, my mom did sit down with a real map and showed us where the Mississippi River was from where we were on the roof. So Geography and math - what an exhausting day for three little kids.

A Place Called Home

I remember a time when we moved to Chicago, and there were 4 of us kids. I was finally allowed to walk to school by myself. It was great because I could walk a different way every day, and I often did. One day, while I was walking home in the alley, I found a $100 bill! What a find! I didn't know what to do. I asked my mom, and she said to think about it because somebody must be missing it. I thought and thought, and my mom suggested we try to find the person who lost it.

So, every day, I went to and from school the same exact way, secretly hoping there was more money out there, laughing every time I went by and found no takers. Everyone else told me to go spend it, but my mom suggested we could ask the police. She called them, and they advised us to come in. We both went to the police station, and they said the detective would hold it for a month. If no one reported it missing, I could keep it! I was so happy; I felt like I was about to burst.

We kept calling every week, feeling like I should call more often, which was absolute agony. Finally, we called, and the policeman told us to come get it because no one had inquired about the lost $100 bill. We skipped to the car and drove home slowly to show it off to the doubters at home. This experience taught me that sometimes patience pays off. My 2 brothers and 2 sisters were envious, so I treated everyone to Peterson's Ice Cream with my beautiful $100 bill. It was a great day for all, and I enjoyed a double dip cinnamon cone more than once, shhh.

Carol L Beers

Memories of My Parents

Then there were all 5 of us kids, Terry, Carol, Linda, Dean, and Les. My Dad was always trying to start his own business; we called him an inventor, but he worked himself through school and said he was now an electrical engineer, whatever that was. He was always home by dinner time and weekends. One time he brought home a cool invention which he called a pickle fork, but no one learned much about how to sell the stuff so on to the next invention. He had a client that needed a better way to grow, trim, and cut down trees. He called it a Tree Monkey. It was a motor with saw blades fixed on, and you put it on the bottom of a tree, and it went round and round trimming to a desired height and really fun to watch.

One time he took us out to drive in a huge parking lot, and each of us got to sit on his lap and steer. My parents were in the PTA at school and put on a real funny play they made up with the other parents for a big audience; it was absolutely hilarious, and we were a big hit at school for a while. For 2 summers in a row, we (all - 7 of us) drove up to Pinelands Lodge in Canada; it was so much fun except for the driving, but my sister Terry found a game hitting each other in the arm with our knuckle! Back and forth until one said give up. Duh…we both got a weird purple bruise on our shoulders and yelled at by the front seat parents.

We were lucky to go to the sand pit where Linda, Dean, and I climbed up and jump/rolled all the way down and jumped into the cold Canadian lake with a pier and a giant tower. Dad said we couldn't go off the tower until we showed him we could swim from a raft to the tower (I later found out he never learned to swim). When my turn came to swim from raft to tower, it was a really long way, and I somehow got water in my mouth but made it about 3 feet from the pier and tower with way too much splashing, spitting, and yelling for help and this great big huge footprint of my dad's hush puppy shoe! I reached for it, and he hauled me in and up on the dock. He was my hero forever. I made many more trips to that pier and even jumped off the highest level into the water with no problems.

Once Dad was having some work done by a contractor and made some stilts for us kids according to our height, and we raced down the driveway. Strawberry knees were far easier to heal than drowning. Our family never seemed to be at a loss for fun things to do. The lessons on swimming and water skiing came the next year.

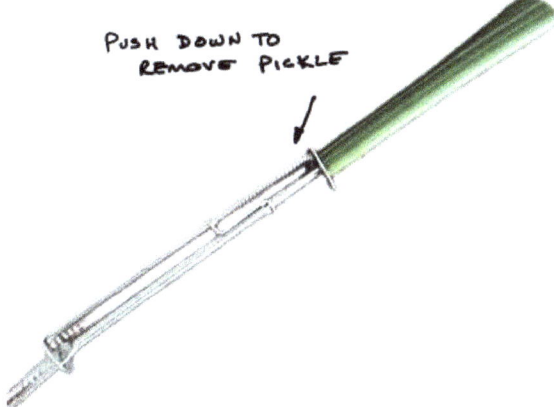

Dad's Pickle Grabber Circa 1955

The Magic of Play

Since our house had the most kids, we had the other kids in the neighborhood come over for games. Kick the can was my favorite. Slip n Slide, hopscotch, stilts races, whiffle ball, all outside, and promptly ended when the street lights went on.

After that, I would try to work on my Girl Scout Badges. Occasionally, I would babysit or do homework. We weren't allowed to watch TV until after supper and only for 2 hours. I was always told to back up on the floor so everyone else could watch. Then not long after that, my teacher sent a note home to my parents that my grades were falling and I should have my eyes examined. I was in the back row and was getting math and reading wrong sometimes. I was the first one in the family called "4 eyes," but I was so happy. I didn't know how bad it was until I got a brand new pair of glasses, and everything was so much better; it was a whole new world, and I loved it!

Giggles and Grins

I think the funniest moment for our family was a joke played on me. At first, I didn't appreciate it, but my Dad decided to involve the rest of the kids.

He informed them of the plan: Mom and Dad would pretend to go outside until the streetlights came on, then sneak down to the basement quietly to hide. Dad went downstairs, and Mom had all the kids hide quietly there as well. Meanwhile, I was tasked with washing the dishes, changing my brother's stinky diapers, and then rinsing them out downstairs. I was so upset, thinking they had forgotten my birthday. Despite my reluctance, I followed their instructions and finally made my way down the long stairway to the basement.

When I reached the bottom of the stairs, everyone jumped out and yelled "Happy Birthday!" Dad captured the moment in pictures, including the messy scene. Initially, I was at my lowest, but then I laid eyes on the most beautiful, gorgeous green bicycle – my first ever! Complete with a horn, pigtails, white wall tires, and a basket. It turned out to be the funniest and most wonderful birthday I had experienced, with everyone laughing in the pictures. Though I may not have fully appreciated it back then, it has become a very cherished memory for all of us. Sometimes, a bit of good- natured mischief can lead to unforgettable moments. That bike remains the greatest gift I've ever received!

Dreams of What I Wanted to Become

When I was in 4th grade, I was in gym class and out on the school playground playing kickball. The ball was heading toward an open-out window, and I ran fast to see if I could catch it so as not to break the window. Instead of catching the ball, I caught my head on the corner of the window and went down hard on the stones below. I don't remember much except there was blood all over, and kids were screaming and yelling for Mr. Brown! He was our gym teacher, and I already had a crush on him. He picked me up and carried me to a couch indoors. He went and got the school nurse to help him figure out what to do. The nurse knew our family was Christian Science because we didn't get shots when the other kids did. So the nurse cleaned and taped my head and called my mom to tell her what happened and that they would bring me home. It turned out the nurse did a great job, and it was the only time I missed school for a day - ever.

As I remember I always had problems with the JFK Fitness Program when doing the ropes I had problems making it to the top. Mr. Brown gave me some secrets about how to use feet, legs, hands and arms in a special way that I was using more muscle and got the top prize.

That is when I decided to become a teacher. I attended 4 colleges (WIU, Triton, SIUE and U of I Chicago) and received 2 degrees, one in education and one in health science. I have been involved in teaching in some form or another ever since. Most people don't go to all the trouble to get a degree, but I did. They just go and get a job. I have no regrets with the length of time it took me to finish college, it was well worth it.

I can still be reminded to this day when I reach up to my head and touch the scar how influenced I was by Mr. Brown's teaching and actions to become a teacher and how important it is to get medical attention when injured, keep others calm in an emergency and to keep an eye on my surroundings! Sometimes you never know what's around you until you get there!

Childhood Lessons that Resonate

I remember a time in 1967 when I was a sophomore, and some of my friends and I were just getting out of school at the day's end. We started heading home when some girls, who called themselves the Greasers, came up behind us. They started talking real loud to drown us out, pushing and shoving, and calling us names. We weren't doing anything except walking too slow. One of them came up to us in front, and I got kicked in the shin hard.

I wanted so bad to get even with a huge kick right back, but then I saw her do it again to another one of us! That was it, and the only thing I could think of to do was to yell - RUN! Our group ran together like a swarm of bees, leaving those kickers far behind. We had some laughs and decided to call ourselves the Doopers for Dear Old Oak Parker's and found another way to walk home. We never saw them again. I'm sure there would have been a nasty mess that day, and we all learned that not fighting sometimes is the very best thing to do! I have always known how to deal with bruises.

Comfort on a Plate

My mom used to make our favorite food on our birthdays. Mine was tuna mornay (noodles with cheese and tuna) or spaghetti with meatballs.

However, my all-time favorite for any meal was eggs. I recall how my mom would have the milkman deliver orange juice, milk, and 144 eggs. I never grew tired of them, and the same goes for the entire family. After the dinner we always got to pick desert and I always picked my favorite blue cake. Delicious always!

My Role Models:
Their Influence and Inspirational Traits

I have had many excellent role models, and gaining experience from them is always a pleasant learning process that molds the best in teamwork. I was picked to be a leader in high school and taught many classes while a junior and senior. During college, I was on the softball team, collegiate volleyball, and field hockey. There is nothing like learning teamwork and watching it truly work for molding great sportsmanship. Most of my favorite teachers made it a fun experience.

While I was a camp counselor teaching fire building, topographical map skills, sailing, canoeing, knots, swimming, and hiking, it made me try to encourage having fun learning. This experience led to forming fond and long-lasting friendships and memories, bringing out the best in all of us. Nothing is better than singing around a campfire; it's quite an unforgettable and inspirational feeling.

Living Through Work

One of my classes in school was called logic. I had a hard time in the beginning, but once I got the idea of it, I began to like it. I never talked or volunteered until the teacher saw my final exam that I got an A+. He wrote on my paper, "You are a diamond in the rough, keep it up." I took his advice, and after getting my college degrees, I started my own business with my brother Les. He was getting his degree, and I was learning how to make sails and custom boat canvas. We found an old potato packing barn in a very good place on the way to Fort Myers Beach, FL. It was so hot those first few years; I remember sweat dripping off my eyebrows and knees.

I had apprenticed for 2 years, and Les came down from Chicago with his wife and son. We opened our business, The Loft Inc. We learned slowly but gradually and had a nice reputation going. Les decided to start his own place and left about 4 years later. I stayed and loved progressing with some new employees. It was a great business, and I loved the work, so many different projects, getting better every day. The business grew, and I was able to buy my own brand new building 2 blocks from the old one.

Finally, I had air conditioning and a computer, and my oldest nephew Jeff as the manager, and enjoyed the good life until he moved back to Chicago, got married, and had a beautiful little girl named Magdalena. They both had great jobs downtown and a wonderful life in the burbs.

After over 30 years of working at one of the greatest jobs in my life where I was the CEO and PRESIDENT of The Loft Inc, I retired and sold almost everything except 2 machines which I used to make stuff for myself and some friends in the garage. I still love to sew and sail.

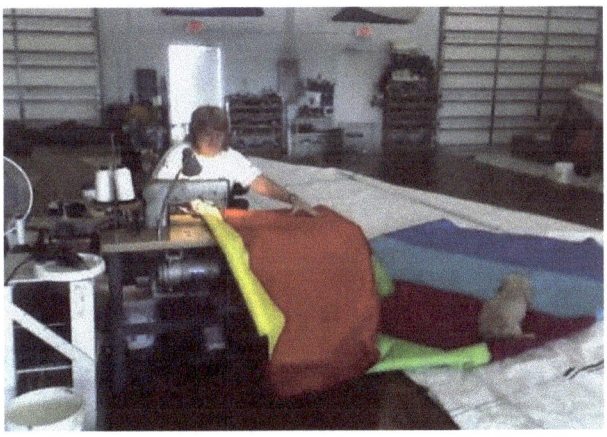

I love to make sails

*Along way from the old potato backing barn where
I started in 1984*

The old Loft (potato packing barn) circa 2002 - Mgr. Jeff Osborne

The Loft Inc. 1984

Delights of Life

There are many things I do for pleasure. I love nature and camping for many years, sailing, carving, photography, candle and soap making, gardening, motorcycle trips, cruises, and engraving. I have gone on many cruises as well as camping with our boat. We went on a rubber raft down the Colorado River camping along the way in the Grand Canyon and stayed at the Bellagio in Las Vegas after. Mixing pleasure, adventure, exploration with relaxing, and meeting new people along the way gives variety to a vacation. It was one of the best vacations!

Carved by hand from local Cypress knees by Carol

Little Wizard sculpted out of clay by Carol

Manatee & Calf sculpted out of clay by Carol

Nature's Serenity or City's Vibrance?

I have had over 23 places to live and 18 jobs in the 10 rough years of my life in both downtown Chicago and a small tent in California, Wisconsin, Utah, Minnesota, and more. So, I pretty much found a wonderful blend of nature and city in Florida in the later years. This is where I learned to make sails for sailboats and started my own business called The Loft Inc for over 30 years. It took a long time to learn how to make sails, but it was very rewarding. The heat was tough because I started in an old potato packing barn with no air conditioning!

Recollecting My Bravest Experience

I made a decision to get sober in Chicago on December 2, 1980. After a year of meetings, I decided to drive out to California with two friends whom I met at AA meetings and while working at a nursing home. Things were going well, and I had a job prospect, so it was a lot of fun. We camped in a little pup tent in the Ortega Mountains. One of my friends left to visit relatives in San Diego, leaving just two of us to head down the mountain to an AA club in Lake Elsinore, CA. We attended meetings, made new friends, and had a great time. One of the members owned a motel and offered us a week's stay in exchange for painting one of the rooms. Everything was going smoothly until my last friend got drunk and decided to head back to Chicago. I hitched a ride back up the mountain to the pup tent alone and spent my time reading and hiking.

After three days, I noticed there weren't many other campers around, but I still had the friends at the club. During one of my hikes, I discovered a large boulder with sunlight at the top. I climbed up, took beautiful pictures, and ended up falling asleep. I woke up to helicopters flying overhead as it was getting dark. I began to climb down when my feet finally touched the ground,

I was confronted with a man holding a rifle aimed at my head. He ordered me to kneel and put my hands over my head and drop my "weapon." I had to make sure to tell him it was a camera, not a gun in my hand. That is when I noticed 10 additional men with rifles slowly come out from behind the trees with rifles aimed right at me. The situation was tense until they realized I was not the one they were looking for. They explained that a person had been killed in the latrine nearby and from the helicopter in the air they mistook me for the actual killer.

After the ordeal, two of the police officers helped me pack up my belongings and escorted me back to the club. I stayed with a friend for the next three days. Then I received a phone call from my Mom. She needed help because she was going to have knee surgery and asked me to come back home to Florida. Without hesitation, I got a plane ticket and flew back to assist my parents. I was immensely grateful for the opportunity to be able to help them and continued to express my gratitude through prayers, including a quirky habit of placing my slippers way under the bed to remind me to kneel twice a day to say thanks, recalling the incident with the camera, the guns and the police.

Ortega Falls: Hiking to a Waterfall Right Off Highway 74

Ortega Falls is a seasonal waterfall off Highway 74 in Lake Elsinore that is only flowing when we get a good rain. During

This where I camped after I got sober and almost got killed

Memories of Personal Excellence

After I got home to Florida, I helped my Mom with her operations and assisted my dad with his meals, which mostly consisted of hamburgers and steak cooked just right until the smoke alarm went off. My Girl Scout badges didn't prepare me much for cooking, except over a campfire. It was decided that I needed to do something besides helping around the house and attending meetings; I needed to find a job.

The first job I found was teaching sailing on the Peace River, about an hour's drive from home. I had bought a '67 Mustang, but it had a cracked block that blew out, so I had to get another car. I found a beautiful '65 orange VW bug with a crack in the floor. The drive was tough, but that wasn't as challenging as the new job itself. I was in charge of teaching adults to sail, mostly vacationers from up north who loved to party every evening after their lesson and I was required to stay until they left.

Being newly sober, it was difficult for me to be around the party scene, especially after a long day and with a long commute home in a less-than- ideal car. Despite the challenges, I fulfilled my duties every day. One memorable day involved a man falling overboard while we were out in a 28' sailboat with four adult students aboard, approaching the Gulf of Mexico.

The man putting up the sail in the bow was half in the bag and slipped on the sail and fell off the boat fully clothed including a huge wool sweater. I immediately grabbed him by his sweater and told the remaining 3 students to toss him the life jacket and keep watching him and pointing at him to make sure he hadn't slipped out of his sweater. I managed to keep a hold of the man, instructing the student at the helm to point the boat up into the wind to slow it down. My hands were becoming sore but I managed to keep a hold while I was making my way aft on the starboard side while climbing over everything. I was yelling to the other students to move to the port side to balance the weight so we didn't all go overboard. As we reached the stern of the boat I yelled at them to grab onto the man to help me get him back in the boat. It happened so fast and I was astonished that it worked so well. With quick thinking and teamwork, we were able to get him back on the boat and return to land safely. We talked about our experience and finally calmed down. The students headed for their rooms to take a nap and I got in my VW and headed home.

The next day I decided to explain to my boss that I could no longer stay for the post-lesson parties. Unfortunately, my boss insisted that if I couldn't participate in the after hours partying I was fired. As I was leaving, the students said they were arranging a congratulation party for that evening and wanted me to attend. I told them I would not be there since I had been fired and we said our fond farewells.

Despite being let go, I was proud of my actions that day. I was glad that my training in man overboard drills from my previous job had prepared me for such a situation. Even though my boss may not have handled the situation correctly, I stood by my decision and was content with the choice I made for myself.

Dad on our 35' sailboat "SEATRECK" with sister Linda at the helm crossing Lake Michigan

Exploring Imperfections:
Desired Changes in Personal Habits

I suppose I should address the elephant in the room now about my 10- year struggle with alcohol. So many things could have been better or not taken as long. My college days were more 'fun' than studying. I went to 4 colleges and took 6 years to complete my 2 degrees. I was the first in my family all the way back to graduate with degrees.

The party was great. There were times when I stopped to earn some money and started up again. My jobs ranged from Jewel bagging, Walmart shoe department, teaching driver education, working on the line soldering electronic parts for phones, and so many others, but I did work every single year of my adult life. No matter how hard I tried, I couldn't stop abusing alcohol. When something bad happened, I would stop for a few days and go again.

Until the last job I got before I got help was at a place called Township for Alcoholism. I was a receptionist and helping others. When I wasn't showing up when I should, they did an intervention on me, helping me get to a detox and 30-day treatment center. The detox was 5 days, and at first, I was strapped to a cot, and nurses came to check on pulse and BP way too often. The place was in a mental institution, and it seemed like an old train station. I remember people screaming and yelling. It wasn't a nice place.

Then I was taken to a rehab which was for 30 days and 30 nights. It was strict with wake up early, help with chores, talks with counselors, reading assignments, meetings with other people, early to bed, no talking. I had problems sleeping and a really nice maintenance man who was sober for 5 years would give me some pointers, and we had some good talks. When I graduated, I found a job at a nursing home, so it was quite a learning process, and I had a bike I rode to and from work every day, even in sub- zero weather in Chicago wind and snow.

This was an uphill climb, and once a few people wanted to go out after work to get to know each other. It was fun till I came back from the bathroom, and a Margarita was sitting in front of me. I was fresh out of treatment and didn't want to be rude, so I sat there and played with the salt at the top, and I was way too close to taking that 'only one drink,' so I gave it to someone else who was very grateful but nowhere near how grateful I was. I went to AA meetings after work, and they advised 90 meetings in 90 days. I worked and went to meetings for a whole year, found a place to live with sober people, and did what the 12 Steps suggested.

So the very best thing I could ever have done was to get sober through the AA program on December 2, 1980. So far so good, not one slip, and still giving it away to keep it. Happiness is Golden.

A few sobriety Medallions from AA

Pivotal Moments of My Life

After I got established as an owner of my own business, things started to settle down, and I bought a used '67 Mustang. My Aunt Heather from Ohio called and asked if her daughter Lisa could come to stay with me after she graduated from college. She wanted to look for a job in Florida and find her own place. I said yes and was glad to help her out. I was really surprised and mostly honored because they knew my past and trusted me implicitly.

It was oh so much fun, and we hung out some. She won the Fort Myers Beach Lounge Lizard Championship by having her picture on a brass bed on the beach with guys fanning and peeling her grapes. I was glad to have her around and watch her grow and learn about life and jobs, etc. She helped me figure things out too. I never had this kind of look at myself until I watched her kind of in my shoes. She still inspires me. I love her dearly.

Carol and Lisa

Unveiling the Most Impactful Decision

I believe that one of the most important decisions in my life was when I met the person who stole my heart. From the first meeting, I knew it would be a lasting friendship. It was in 1988, and we both had jobs to keep us busy and friends who lived with us, so we usually went places with 2-4 other friends.

There was one time camping at the Lykes Brothers Campground along the silver river with a canoe. We fished and caught quite a few, hanging them off the stern. The river was very winding and confusing to know which way to go, so we took off our socks to mark the way, often hanging our feet in the water. It started to rain, so we collected our wet socks on the way back and made way for our camp and dinner over an open fire. When we got back and pulled the boat out of the water, the string of fish was nothing but bones and heads. A big alligator was eating them the whole time we were there, and I'm so glad we didn't go for a swim and our toes didn't look like bait.

After a couple of years, we decided to buy a house together. The rest is history! Her name is Susan, and she is the most important person and the decision that helped set the trajectory of my life. We have lived together since then and actually got married when the government voted to allow same-sex marriage in November 2013. We had a celebration in New York where she was from, and then another celebration in Chicago where my family is from, and of course the last one in Florida where we live.

We have gone on many cruises together and have both retired, so now our life is less complicated, and we are still so happy together.

Carol and Sue dressed up for "Ribeye" on Viking cruise

Exploring Significant Figures in My Life

When I moved to Florida, I resided with my parents. After my sailing lessons, I dedicated my time to searching for a new job. A man, Captain Al, four years sober, guided me to beach meetings and encouraged me to attend an additional 90 meetings in 90 days for support. He connected me with individuals involved in sailing, hinting at a potential job opening.

Equipped with the address and contact details, I visited the location. The manager inquired about my sailing experience, prompting me to recount my involvement since the age of 15. When asked about sewing, I shared my limited experience, including earning Girl Scout badges for sewing and crafting an apron in sixth grade.

During the tour of the sailing store, the manager showcased a vast 50x30 wood varnished floor where boat sails were crafted. I was amused by the sight of large metal sewing machines. Sitting down, he demonstrated sewing a 6 and provided me with guidance. Before leaving, he requested that I sew a 5 on a piece of material for evaluation the next morning. Determined, I spent an hour perfecting the task, returning promptly the following day to learn that I was hired.

Unbeknownst to me at the time, this job marked the inception of my entrepreneurial journey. Over the next 30 years, I transitioned from an apprentice to the CEO of my corporation. Initially, I worked alongside my brother Les, eventually branching out on my own. Hiring staff, including Matt, who departed after a year, and later Tim, a retired preacher, who brought joy to the workplace. Despite various challenges, I managed the business until my retirement, cherishing the memories created with remarkable individuals seeking custom boat canvas fabrication and sails.

My years involved diverse projects, from crafting machine gun covers for Coast Guard boats to sewing elaborate designs like a fire-breathing dragon on a sail. Requests ranged from custom safety harnesses for zip- lining to intricate biminis for large powerboats. Reflecting on the multitude of specialized boat enclosures and unique creations, including a canoe made by bending a soft sided metal frame and fastening a vinyl skin to it, I realized my deep-rooted passion for the craft and the satisfaction it brought me over the years.

Me and cousin Ricky

You name it, I tame it.

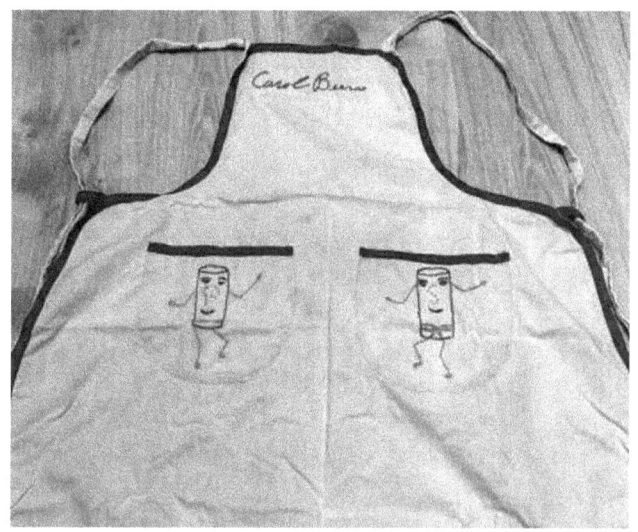

My 6th grade sewing project that started a 30 year occupation

Story of a Happy Wanderer

There was one time a bunch of us teachers got together for a cruise in Alaska. It was one of the most awesome and picturesque places I've ever been to. When we first got there, we stayed at the Alyeska Resort for the night and then split into small groups the next morning. I went on a hike by myself with a sandwich and rain jacket along a beautiful fast-moving river. There were so many great things to see – bald eagles catching fish, people paddling in a zodiac, and even a bear feeding her cub. It started to rain, and most of us got back pretty fast.

We were making plans to go up the giant ski mountain on the tram the next day before leaving to go by bus to the cruise ship. About 6 of us inquired about walking down the ski mountain and were all told it wouldn't take much longer than 45 minutes to an hour. So we went up for a spectacular view on the tram, and when we got out to go for the hike, there was only one person that showed up – that was me. Even my best friend decided we both had phones and they would go back down on the tram in case something happened.

So, I left and started down singing 'Happy Wanderer,' and up came a small stream and some construction – I guess they were repairing something. So, I made my way through and around the fast-moving stream because it was at much more of a decline. I had to start making my path more of an S-shape than straight down this ski hill. The next thing that happened was the fog came rolling in and became so thick I could hardly see in front of me. I called my best friend, and there was no reception.

I took a little rest and got going again. When the fog started to lift, there on my left about 50 feet away was a moose and her baby calf, just staring at me. I wasn't sure who was going to charge first, and I had to get back down the mountain before the bus took off and the cruise ship left without me. So, I found a thin branch and tied my red scarf to the top and waved it up high as I started down again!

My friend had found a ranger, and the closer I got, the better the reception was. The ranger told me to raise and wave the stick so he could find me. As he came up in his truck, I saw the town and waved like crazy! I got in the truck, and we passed another moose – yikes, glad I was on my way back to the bus, which was parked waiting. I made it and even had 5 minutes until the bus was leaving.

When we got to the ship, we all took a nap, and they were going to meet at the bar before dinner. I went to the deserted casino. For the next 45 minutes, I hit 4 machines for almost $3800.00. I ran up to the bar to show the teachers my payout, and I was totally forgiven for my risky trip. The funny thing was, three of them wanted 'lessons' on how I won. I just said, put money in, pull the arm, and hope you get lucky, and remember to only use money you can afford to lose. The next 4 days, I was learning about the consequences – the pain in my legs told me quite loudly. But I would do it again in a heartbeat.

Carol Mount Alyeska Alaska

Revisiting the Most Profound Event

In the 1960s, I was active in protests and trying to join people in helping our country remember the constitution and, above all else, to not engage in anger or violence. I was back in Chicago, and it was filled with violence. The Vietnam War was really messing with everyone's head.

During summers, I was camping with kids in Wisconsin, so I was able to average out the anger and joy. I have always been involved in the Girl Scouts. There is nothing more heart warming than to see the look on a kids face when you have taught them a new skill such as: lighting a fire without a match, tying a Bowline knot and it's purpose, or doing the breast-stroke in the water because it's the most relaxing stroke. It is such a joy to watch the kids burst with pride and happiness when they succeed.

Then, with summer over, I experienced walking across the campus at WIU and seeing U.S. troops on top of the buildings. I have always wondered why people can't just strive to be happy. That is when I truly became aware that life is a balance of opposites: love vs hate, kindness vs cruelty, good vs evil, happiness vs sadness and anger vs peacefulness. It is up to me to choose the path I walk.

Peace and Love

A Habit Vital to Daily Life

The habit I worked on every day was the Serenity Prayer: "God, grant me the serenity to accept the things I cannot change, the courage to change the things I can, and the wisdom to know the difference." This practice centers me daily, sometimes even more frequently. Additionally, I strive to perform a daily act of kindness and live by the 12 steps of the AA program. I contribute to the program by having my information in the world directory, leading meetings, and sponsoring individuals affectionately referred to as "pigeons."

I believe there are no simple steps to a wonderful life, but if you truly commit, it does work and brings a lifetime of rewards. The key is to give away what you have to maintain it. At the time of writing this book, if I continue on this path for the next few months, I will reach 45 years (December 2, 1980) since my last drink. I find myself happier than I ever imagined possible, and I am certain that without this journey, I might not be alive today.

Pearls of Wisdom:
Incorporating Vital Life Lessons

I would like to think that the Golden Rule, "Do unto others the way you would have them do unto you," would be the best and first life lesson. It would help a lot to be your own best friend in order to do that.

It also took me a long time to learn that to listen is a necessity no matter who you're talking to. Use your words well, think before you talk because most of the time you can't take it back and you might regret it. Always tell the truth; the older you get, the harder it is to remember what you said - you never forget the truth.

Avoid people that you don't trust or have hurt others. Make sure to have some humility (bragging is a really bad look). Be aware of your surroundings and be careful. Most of all, try your best to be happy.

My Life's Biggest Challenge

It's with mixed feelings if my biggest challenge was the best or not. My brother and I started a business, and times were tough, but slowly we built it up, and we were making pretty good money. Then came the time when my brother wanted to have his own business. I couldn't quite figure out why, but I learned that some things I don't need to know. Someone said we killed the goose that laid the golden egg!

We all have our troubles, and I can only say that when we separated, it was one of the toughest times in my life. But I'm grateful because at my most lost time, it forced me to get serious about my work life and get tough alone. It truly helped me get stronger and more serious about it or find something else. This challenge dared me to do better. It took a while, but I did get better and stronger and found myself forgiving and feeling better than ever.

My Happiest Life Moment

One of the happiest and significant times in my life is when my Dad asked to take me out to dinner! This never happened before, so I almost thought I did something wrong. We went to a really nice restaurant and talked about our work mostly. He told me a little story of when he was a small boy and his Mom (my grandma) told him to go get the wagon and get your Dad home. It was something he did quite often because the bartender called the house and said to come get him. So my Dad had to go to the local Tavern in Detroit, go in to get him in the wagon, and get him home. I was sure this story was very meaningful to him because there was a tiny tear in his eye.

My dad stood up and motioned to the waitress to come over, and she brought over a beautiful little cake with 10 candles on it to signify the 10- year anniversary of my sobriety. It was the first and last time we spoke about it, except when he asked me if I could have a meeting with his Boss because he was in trouble with alcohol. I was happy to help. Very proud and very happy.

Recounting My Most Heartbreaking Moment

One of the most heartbreaking moments in my life was when my Mom passed away. A nurse informed me that her time was near, and I rushed out of the hospital room to a window. There, a kind lady approached me, asking if I was okay. I couldn't hold back my tears as I replied that my mom was dying that day. The stranger embraced me tightly, offering words of comfort, saying, "It will get better."

My mom suffered from rheumatoid arthritis, a condition that caused her immense pain and limited her mobility. Both my parents were on the verge of fulfilling a ten-year dream of building a 52-foot boat and exploring new places. Unfortunately, shortly after completing the boat, my mom had to undergo surgeries to replace three knees and two hips, with one knee getting infected.

I tried my best to juggle everything, but the weight of the situation was overwhelming. Looking back, I regret not spending more time with her, even though she made an effort to visit me whenever possible. At that time, I was managing my own company located in an old potato packing barn without air conditioning, making it challenging for my mom to visit frequently. However, she did lend a helping hand when I underwent surgery and occasionally brought me lunch, showing her love and thoughtfulness.

My mom was the epitome of kindness and love, and witnessing her in pain was truly heart-wrenching. Despite my desire to alleviate her suffering, all I could do was shower her with love and care.

Me and Mom playing darts

In the Grip of Fear

I remember a scary time once when I was working on a charter fishing boat to earn extra money for school. We had taken a party of 4 (2 fathers and 2 teenagers). The trip had been postponed 2 times before, so we were determined to get this show on the road. They had promised fresh fish to many. It was a cold day in October, probably the last day before the harbor closed. The temperature outside was 42°F, and the Lake Michigan water temp was 37°F (on the top of the water). For sure, the last trip this boat would take this year!

We went out about 15 miles and put down the lines with big treble hooks to see what we might get. After many unsuccessful attempts, changes had to be made like the depth we would go for, the water temperature, or the bait, so we kept trying. Two hours of changing everything, and I finally decided to put on our "lucky song" called The Old Lamp Lighter! Not 2 minutes later, we got a hit! The line went buzzing, and the teenager had caught his first Chinook Salmon. This fish usually doesn't come down south of Canada, and it was a 28-pounder! Right here in Chicago! Everyone on board was jumping for joy when the other line clicked and started buzzing, and the father grabbed the line and reeled in a huge 34- pounder Coho salmon.

We hit the jackpot and got things cleaned up and re-rigged all 4 lines again. Now we were making a slow turn trying to head back because it was getting colder, and the line started buzzing again! This time it took longer, and the other teenager worked the fish till his father gave him a rest and finished bringing in the most beautiful and rare Brown Trout that weighed 46 pounds. The one father said this was suitable for the taxidermist. So we headed back to the Yacht Club with the fish and myself on ice.

After backing up to the club, we could see there was a crowd forming in the nice warm club all across the long windows. The Captain started cleaning the fish starting with the lightest one. By the time he got to the heaviest, he held it up to the people in the gallery and all around the shore, and all of a sudden, his hand slipped and dropped the prize Brown Trout into the water, and we all watched it slowly disappear to the bottom of Lake Michigan. Everyone just stood in shock silently wondering what to do next.

This was back in the '70s before I quit drinking, and people were coming down offering brandy and vodka. This is when my Captain asked if I could get it. The depth was 26 ft, and the temperature about 34°F. That's when I decided to change into my shorts and shirt and see if I could get it. One of the guys offered a mask, and down I went. It was dark and cold, with lots of tree limbs from a recent storm, but no sign of the star of the show, that beautiful Brown Trout. I was so sure it would sparkle, but I couldn't find it.

Up I went as fast as I could with not much air to spare. I took a rest and a few more shots of brandy and decided to make one last try. This time, I went straight down and started rummaging through the tree limbs when I caught my watch and arm in a tree limb and started to struggle and panic a little because I couldn't move it away. The only thing I could think of was to remember my training at the YMCA when I got my WSI Water Safety Instructor Certification with my Brother Dean.

I calmed down and gave my decidedly last try and planted my feet on the ground and with the last breath of air and the only frozen strength my hands had left, I saw the sparkle! There it was, the prize fish! I grabbed it and pushed up with everything I had left and went straight up toward the surface of the water thinking, please God, just a few more seconds. I broke the surface and felt many hands and arms grab both me and the fish, wrap me with blankets, and make sure I was conscious. It was very memorable and probably the closest I've ever been to dying. The story is still told about that day even to this day.

Brown Trout caught in Lake Michigan at Chicago Oct. 1973

What I Wish My Loved Ones Knew

I'm thinking about the first back-to-back 2-week cruise I've ever been on. It was supposed to be a 30-day cruise on the Viking ship Star, a cruise from Scandinavia to Spain. Sue's brother Rich and sister-in-law Joanne gave it to us as a retirement present. We started out flying to Stockholm, Sweden, then got on this beautiful ship to Helsinki, Finland, and St.

Petersburg, Russia. On the way to Estonia, Sue and I were at the back of the ship and noticed something strange with the wake. As we watched from the transom, the starboard engine seemed to have something terribly wrong. You could barely feel the engine slow, and the wake of this 745 ft x 94 ft ship started to look different from the port engine's aft. It was obvious that there was a problem. The ship had severe engine problems and had to hobble on to our next stop in Tallinn, Estonia. It was beautiful to me, but many people on board were furious and wanted to leave immediately by plane, helicopter, or fishing boat. They were not happy, but we sure were. Everyone had meetings on board about what to do, and our vote was 3-1 to keep going. Just think, over half of them left! We almost had the entire ship to ourselves. Later I saw where they had cut a huge hole in the hull to remove and replace the broken engine. Wow, what a job!

The excursions were figured out on the spur, so we went to places no one had gotten to go before. My most favorite was a bike ride all around the town of Tallinn. We stopped our bikes to rest in the back of a little church. There were huge statues of Russian soldiers all broken on the ground. This is what they did after Russia had tried to take over all of Estonia. They were free after the war and put the town back to the charming storybook cobblestone city it used to be. There were even little sailboats practicing for the Olympics. When we left Estonia, we went to Poland, and somehow the ship was granted the only ever passage of a cruise ship through the Kiel Canal between Denmark and Germany. What a treat with the incredible courage and dedication from the Captain and Crew of the Viking Star. There were so many moments that could have ended this most memorable, unique, incredible journey never to be equaled and never to be forgotten. I felt so lucky and grateful.

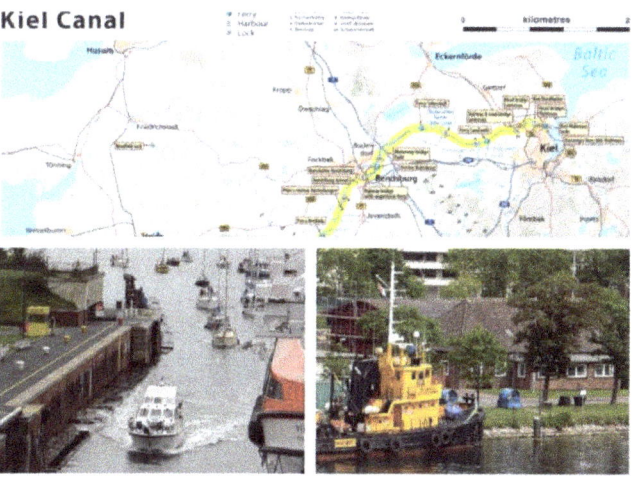

Carol L Beers

My Greatest Achievement

They say life's greatest accomplishments and areas of pride come from things that seem totally impossible.

Having made it through 17 hurricanes, survived, and rebuilt both my business and home. One day at a time stacked up 162,85 days as of right now of good sober living. Okay, this one is weird, saved $81,429.62 quitting smoking in 2000 with okay lungs so far. An incredible trip on a submarine down 275 ft in Lake Superior. Walked on the face of a statue of Stalin laying down broken in a churchyard in Tallinn, Estonia after Russia left their country and all the Russian statues were taken down. Teaching kids 8-18 how to sail at Colombia Yacht Club for 4 years on Lake Michigan. Of course, there is more, but it all totals up to a sense of self- assurance and a positive self-perception.

Milton

Rethinking Choices and Unexplored Paths

I regret that my mom passed away before I could share the news of my upcoming marriage with her. Despite not verbalizing it for years, I believe she had an inkling. It would have brought her joy, as she always wished for the happiness of all her five children. I was certain she could sense my profound happiness. When I eventually disclosed the news to my dad, he didn't acknowledge the invitation. Nonetheless, we celebrated in three different states due to our dispersed family and friends. The gatherings were filled with joy, and it was heartwarming to reunite with some of our long-time friends.

Mom was gentle, loving and kind!

Friendship That Withstood Time

I was fortunate enough to reconnect with one of my favorite people from high school after about a 10-year gap. Our friendship resumed once her kids were grown, and work was less demanding. Maureen and I were not only high school and college buddies but also camping companions and fellow counselors at Camp White Deer in Wisconsin. Finding her in the same house she grew up in was heartwarming. We've embarked on trips together, reminiscing about the good old days, often laughing so hard that we'd nearly collapse.

Most importantly, we've delved into discussions about politics and other significant matters, sharing insights like-minded individuals do. It's comforting to know that I can reach out to her anytime for help or just to chat – the bond we share has only grown stronger over time. Thank you, Maureen, for giving our enduring long-distance friendship a second chance. You truly are the best.

My friend Maureen

Managing Trust's Shattered Bonds

Yes, I have experienced betrayal, one from family, two from friends, and one from a professional. In my life's experience, I have been taught well to obey the Golden Rule. If others dump, disrespect, or betray my trust, I should absolutely change my playground and playmates. I deserve respect and kindness as well as I give it. There are loads of wonderful people, and nothing says we should not seek them out to have a better future of happiness always.

Our dogs are constant smile makers can

Feeling Loved and Embraced

There is no doubt I did know the moment I felt loved and understood. A friend introduced me to my Susan (I say "my Susan" because we knew a lot of Susans back in 1989.) We had dinner and talked like we were old friends, and she actually listened and paid attention. There was a beautiful twinkle in her eyes and a smile that melted me. Considering she was a nurse, I should have figured out some of her earlier, but she had a really gentle way about her that was refreshing. I had never felt that way before or since, even after dating.

When we had free time, we were together as much as possible. We would watch a Cubs game or ride our Harley motorcycles to places we had never been, mostly in Florida. We would go camping by the river or to friends' homes to play games, or out on our boat. Sometimes visiting friends or relatives in Pa., Chicago, NY, it was great getting to know each other. It was hard to have to go home or to go to work. The time together was just like floating on the water. It was smooth and wonderful. Sometimes it felt like we had known each other forever.

The Start of Us

Susan and her friend were vacationing in Florida and a mutual friend invited us to dinner at the local Chinese restaurant. During their visit we hung out together several times and got to know each other. We continued to stay in touch after Susan returned to New York.

Since Susan visited Florida frequently she decided to build a house in Fort Myers. We called and wrote each other frequently during this period as I was keeping an eye on the house construction and updating her on the progress. When the house was finally finished Susan decided to relocate to Florida permanently. This was the start of us!

We saw each other often and went on many wonderful camping trips and vacations together. About 2 years later we each sold our house and bought a wonderful home together. We moved in with our 2 little puppies Harley and Cassie where we have enjoyed our lives together for over 30 years. Who could ever have dreamed this? It was a miracle.

Sue & Carol dogsledding on Alaska Glacier

Sue & Carol in Gibraltar at the WW II Caves

The Happiness Found in Children's Smiles

I was always aware of safety, especially around kids. My kids were my own 2 brothers and 2 sisters, then student teaching in grade school and high school and at a school in downtown Latin School of Chicago. Every summer, I taught sailing, canoeing, and camping. The offer came to teach in New Zealand! But I turned them both down and went to California for a chance at teaching big boat sailing. Then my parents needed me to come down to Florida to help take care of my Mom.

The best times with the kids seem to be that I will always remember teaching them the simplest things from tying shoes to a great tennis serve, the sparkle in their eyes after "they got it," the smile and proud acknowledgment they had learned and knew something they would never forget, pride through practice and accomplishment. So all of 'my kids' have and always will bring tremendous joy and happiness and will maybe even pass it on as I did with Mr. Brown.

Treacy, Ethan and Mara

Rowen, Rainer and Carol

Michael and Carol

The Challenges of Working with Kids

Some of the most challenging moments in my life were when I was teaching kids aged 8-18 sailing at Colombia Yacht Club (1976-1980) in downtown Chicago on Lake Michigan. All the kids in the class, usually 10-20, would gather around on the afterdeck of the Yacht Club. I would teach them nomenclature, help them get familiar with each other, and then we would head to the docks. There, I explained how to wear their life jackets every time they were in boats or around them. They had to pass a short swim test, and I was relieved that I had passed my own test with WSI - Water Safety Instructor.

Everything was going well as we got the boats in and out of the water until the Police came by and warned us that the school next door to our club had an emergency. One of the students had been hit and knocked out by the boom of a boat. This incident was a shock because in my four years of teaching in this position and these waters, the worst accident had been a boy getting hit with a ball after lunch. After cleaning up and having lunch, I noticed someone was missing. My face turned red, and I felt impending doom. I had to make sure, so I ran downstairs and found my kid in the bathroom, at least it wasn't him.

Later, when the parents got the news that someone was hurt, we reassured them that it wasn't from our class but from the next class down the way. My Mom and Dad came down to see if the rumor that I was dead was true. The horror of not knowing was evident on their faces, but we all took deep cleansing breaths, hugged, cried happy tears, and dismissed with a promise of coming back tomorrow. It was a wonderful summer for all of us, something I'll never forget. It emphasized that safety is the most important quality to remember when on or around the water.

Columbia Yacht Club, Carol and Magdalena

Chasing Dreams

I learned about the Desiderata many years ago and try to read it as often as possible. The suggestions provide me with a path and give me strength, hope, knowledge, calmness, honesty, and all the qualities anyone could benefit from by striving to be happy. And yes, I surely am.

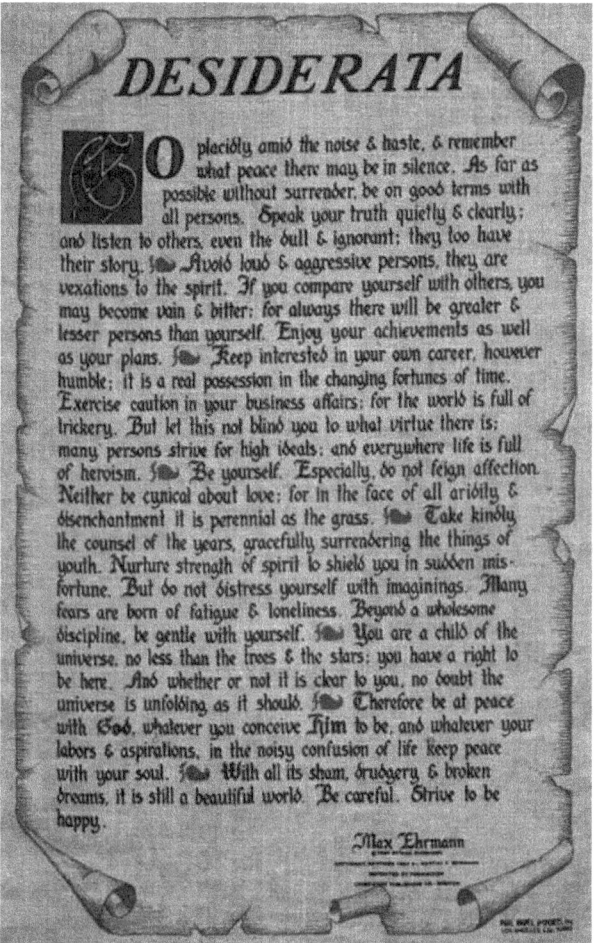

Favorite Wall Hanging

Personal Paradise

I took numerous cruises and the favorite place I visited was Tallinn, Estonia. I always had a dream to take the family on the boat my Dad built (a 52' trawler named Tenure). The name "Tenure" came from the fact that it took my dad 10 years to build the boat himself. It was to be my dream trip with other like-minded boat owners, ending up at Estonia. The little city of Tallinn is like a fairytale with cobblestone streets, castle like buildings and the friendliest people I've ever met. The country has been taken over by the Russians several times and reclaimed after the people revolted and had the return of their peaceful country.

It was a shame we never got to fulfill the dream before my parents passed on. However, I do hope Sue and I might one day fly back to our favorite place in the friendly town of Tallinn. Ideally it would be during the Tallinn Song Festival which occurs every 5 years over three days and is one of the largest choral gatherings in the world. The band shell holds up to 15,000 singers at one time.

The Tallinn Band Shell we visited on our bike tour.

"Tenure" Built by Howard L Beers

Wishing for a Different Path Taken

I've thought about this question a lot, and the only answer I keep coming up with is that it took every single thing in my life to get me where I am now - the good, the bad, and the ugly. All the people I came to like or not, all the roads not taken, and all the most wonderful things I've been able to take part in (which I could never have even dreamed of). I can't express enough how I believe and try to live my life by "Doing unto others as I would like to have done unto me." Just a smile or an acknowledgment of something good every day, whether it's a friend, family, or stranger, can actually affect the outcome of life and it's better to have it be in a positive direction than not. So I would not change a thing.

Choosing One Day to Relive in a Time Machine

I would go back to spend more time with my Mom on her last day. I was able to be with her for a little while, but it seemed so helpless. I leaned over, and she squeezed my hand as if to say, "Don't worry, it will all be ok." My helplessness was eased a little, and I let her know it's ok to let go. She would never be in pain again.

I would have liked to spend time with my brother Dean in his last days. My brother Dean was one of the bravest of the kids, and we didn't even know how bad he had gotten until close to the end. I couldn't have gone anyway because I had Covid. But we pretty much knew how much we would miss each other when he gave a beautiful speech for Sue and me at our Marriage Ceremony.

My Mom Nancy and me

Embracing the Signs of Aging

Growing old, to me, is a relative process. Do old people walk 12,373 steps in a day? Or hike 4.96 miles? Do old people strap themselves into a harness in the World's Largest Zipline at 5330 ft. with a vertical drop of 1350 ft. at 60 MPH in Hookah, Alaska? I did on 07/10/2013.

Do old people take a tram up a ski mountain to 3,939 ft altitude to hike down solo? Come on... we don't notice getting old; we work hard to avoid it!

Life in Three Words

Happy, Grateful, and Free. I would say this whole Memoir So Far has been an incredible journey of self-reflection. My hopes are that my friends and family can understand this is written for me to feel better about myself and that any reader can maybe read it with an open mind and try to balance a life well-lived by mixing the most scary with the very most happy, grateful and free moments because that's what life's all about.

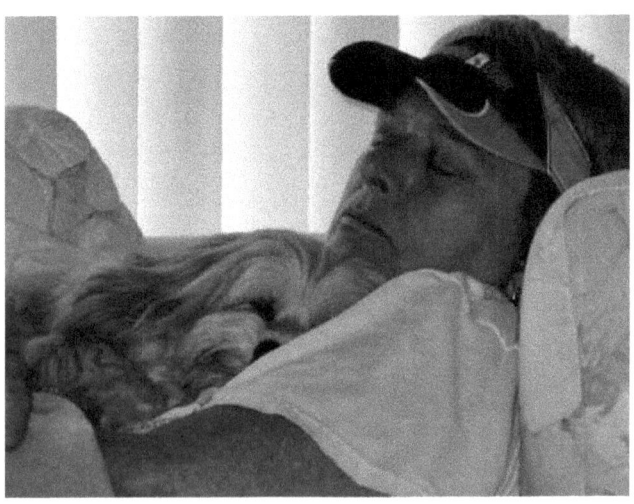

How I Wish to Be Remembered

This is a difficult question to answer because I've always believed that if you have to tell someone how great you are, then you probably aren't. I strive to live a life filled with spreading happiness and love wherever possible. I aim to be the best version of myself, staying positive even when talking to myself, as self-affirmation is beneficial in moderation.

I prioritize safety by being vigilant for any potential harm, including negative language and attitudes. I value honesty, integrity, and kindness in my interactions with family and friends. I remind myself to take moments to breathe deeply and enjoy the sunshine. It's important to prioritize sleep and practice calming techniques like deep breaths or counting to ten when feeling upset. Always remember that you are loved.

Helicopter ride to Glacier in Alaska

Biltmore Estates in Asheville

Passing the Torch

Get your education and have some fun. Find a place you like better than any other place. Find something to do that you like doing the most. Find a person you love the most to share the first two with! Oh yes, don't forget to make some wonderful friends that have a bond with your honesty, trust, serenity, wisdom, and acceptance. Life can be the most wonderful thing if you work hard at achieving it always!

Make sure to stay healthy and get skin checks since skin cancer runs in our family. Try not to get caught up with the ones that want to hold you back because you can do anything you want. Try to learn and respect your elders they have so much experience, and wisdom of the ages and won't be around as long as you to pass it on so cherish them while you can.

6 Pack Sub 283' below surface

Recognizing Those I'm Most Thankful For

I am most thankful to my Mom and Dad. They were always there and truly loved all 5 of us, but I always felt special, proud, and lucky to have them most of my life.

My teacher in 5th grade read all of the Laura Ingles Wilder books, all about the tough times on the Prairie, where you could still be happy and go through bad times. Another book she gave me to read was "My Side of the Mountain," which was about a kid who studied hard, learned about camping and self-sufficiency, and spent a year away from home by himself.

My Triplets aunts & uncle were fun. Helen, Heather, and Tim all spent time with us when we were growing up. Some were inspiring, and some showed what not to do, but all in all, they had good hearts and made it really fun.

In college, there were many courses that made a difference, such as psychology, anatomy, physiology, and education. The professionals who helped me in detox and treatment gave me the 12 Steps of AA, helping me learn a way of life that brought me serenity and happiness. I continue to meet many more people today whom I'm sure are the right ones. It took going through the rough times to show me the way not to go.

Seeking Reconciliation and Closure

One Friday afternoon, a man entered my shop at the Loft and asked if I could do a rush order to repair a sail for a 37 ft sailboat he was working on as a cabinet maker. His name was Chip, and he needed it by Sunday morning. The sail was in bad shape, requiring a lot of work and material to patch it up correctly. I explained that I would need to spend out of pocket for the special material and overtime for me and my helper if I could get him to stay late. After ensuring I could meet the time and financial commitments, we agreed that he would pay half in cash upfront and the reminder in cash when he came to pick up the sail. Chip paid me half in cash and swore he would be back Sunday morning at 8 am to pick up the sail and pay the remaining balance.

Well, Chip arrived 3 hours late on Sunday and without any cash. I was not happy! He was waving a credit card that wasn't his and smelled like a brewery. I told him this was not the deal, you are late and do not have the cash. He began yelling, swinging his arms and ran to the back of the shop to look for his sail. I told him he couldn't have it. He grabbed the sail and I told him I was calling the cops. We struggled with the huge, heavy sail and

I refused to let it go. Chip kept trying to pull it away when the cops arrived. I was lucky they were only 2 blocks away. He grabbed me by my neck with both hands. I dropped the sail and fell down as the cops apprehended him. The cops said they would return later to take my statement. I'm not sure how things finally ended up.

I did not see Chip again for a while when one day he came to the shop and wanted to apologize. He said he felt bad about what happened and he was in AA, 40 days sober, and doing better. I told him I was not ready to accept his apology and did not want to see or hear from him again.

After a while I looked for him at AA meetings to tell him I hoped he was still sober. A man who knew Chip came into the shop one day and told me he had sold everything and moved away.

In hindsight, I regret not hearing him out, as it might have eased the fear I harbored from the past. Nevertheless, I've come to realize that dwelling on the past doesn't serve me well. Forgiveness, in the end, is liberating for everyone involved.

Acts of Kindness in My Heart

Acts of kindness I've received that still warm my heart;

The warm huge hug from a complete stranger when my Mom died. My Mom and Dad giving me a sailboat when I graduated High School. My friends giving me a surprise birthday party at 60.

My cousin Lisa giving me an ok when she hugged me and said everything will be ok.

My cousin Matt when he helped me when I needed it and always brightened my day.

My bro Dean for thinking and saying I was great. My bro Les for starting a business with me.

My friends from the program who stuck in there no matter what. My sisters Linda and Terry for trying.

My spouse Susan for being there with a hug or any answer and my best friend.

The Book Title of My Life

Learning to be my own best friend - Life's lessons on becoming my own best friend - A MEMOIR SO FAR... I'm definitely not done.

Always Look for the Rainbow

Message to Loved Ones

There are so many things more I wanted to say and so many things I have learned from knowing all of you. I guess I'll have to ask anyone who reads this to please let me know if you could stand another one before I go? If you have time all I can say is maybe write it in the spare places you can find in the book and sign your name and feel free to share it with others and enjoy.

This Memoir started out as a kind of dare and decidedly turned out to be really fun thinking about all the great times we all had together and the overcoming of obstacles and maintaining the love we always have had for each other. I thank you from the bottom of my heart. CLB

Cubs vs Marlins at Jet Blue Park

Feelings That Unveiled in Remembering Life

I am very surprised by how much writing this book has helped me understand myself better. It has allowed me to forgive and recognize the proud moments in the life that I have been given. I may not be perfect, but at least there was a learning curve, and I did get better every day. I truly thank all the relatives, friends, and readers that stayed with me along the way, putting up with my frailties, faults, and fun because we really did have them all.

Love, CB

My evening walking companion - no better feeling